I0528673

ANNIE AND NOAH'S GREAT SUMMER ADVENTURE TO YELLOWSTONE NATIONAL PARK

Written By Jessie Hartel

Copyright © 2024 Jessie Hartel
All rights reserved.
No portion of this book may be
reproduced in any form without written
permission from the publisher or author
except as permitted by U.S. copyright
law.

DEDICATION

This Book is dedicated to my husband Shawn and daughter Lilly who make my life so much brighter. I am very thankful for all of the time that they sacrificed to allow me to do so many amazing things that enrich all of our lives.

Annie and Noah are just beginning their first week of summer vacation. They are waiting for Dad to get off of work so that they can start packing for their family vacation. This year's great adventure is to Yellowstone National Park in Wyoming.

The car is all packed and everyone is ready to go. Mom puts the family dogs, Elvis and Johnny in the car and away they go.

"I see Nevada", says Noah. "I see California", says Dad. License plate bingo is the family's favorite game on long-distance road trips. After an hour of driving Annie asks, "Are we there yet?" "No", says Mom as she smiles at Annie.

After hours of road bingo, a nap, and a pit stop at a gas station for goodies, the family finally makes it to the cabin in Yellowstone National Park. Annie, Noah, and Mom all get out of the car to see the beautiful view of the Grand Tetons and the herd of buffalo in the distance.

Meanwhile, Dad is unpacking the luggage from the car and putting it into the cabin
"I call top bunk", says Annie. "No, I called top bunk back in the car", says Noah. Dad makes Annie and Noah flip a coin to see who gets to sleep on the top bunk and Annie wins.

The whole family works together to unpack their suitcases and pack their hiking packs for the next day. Everyone is exhausted from the long drive and so they all say their good-night-sleep-tights and head to bed. An adventurous vacation is on their minds as they fall asleep.

"Good morning, I have eggs and bacon ready for the first person who gets dressed", says Mom. Of course, everyone jumps out of bed to race each other to the first plate of Mom's delicious cooking.

With tummies all full and hiking bags packed, they begin their morning hike in formation as Dad whistles an old Air Force tune. Elvis and Johnny are in the lead and off they go up into the mountain trail. They stop by the Ranger station before they begin their hike so that Dad can give the Ranger the hiking plan. Then off they went to begin their amazing adventure.

As the family is walking Annie hears a noise and says, "Do you hear that rattling noise?" Dad takes a listen and says, "That is a rattlesnake, they are very dangerous so make sure that we are walking away from that noise."

As they continue on Mom sees a beaver building a dam in the river. She says, "Kids look at the beaver, it is collecting sticks and branches to build itself a safe home called a dam, how amazing that we get to see this."

Just around the corner past a large group of trees, Noah sees the most beautiful waterfall and says "look guys- look!" Dad looks at the map and says, "This must be hidden falls." "I think this is a great place to have lunch," says Mom. "I will get the sandwiches ready," says Noah. "I will get the picnic blanket laid out," says Annie.

"Well, that was a great lunch with a beautiful view," says Mom. "Are we ready to hike and set up camp at Jenny Lake?" At the same time, everyone replied, "Let's do it."

After a couple of miles into their hike, Annie notices a bear off in the far distance. "Everyone needs to start shaking their jingle bells so that we do not startle the bears," says Mom. Dad pulls out the map and identifies that the bear looks like a grizzly bear because of the extra hump on his back. "Come on let's keep going and making loud noises so that the bears will run off."

At about dusk the family finally makes it to Jenny Lake. "How amazing and beautiful this is," says Mom. Dad pulls out the tent and stakes teaching Annie how to build a tent while Mom is teaching Noah how to skip rocks on the lake..

Once Dad and Annie got the tent set up, Mom and Noah gathered twigs, sticks, and small logs for their fire. Mom put a hot dog on a stick for each one of us. "So, what was everyone's favorite part of the day," asks Dad. "I loved watching the beaver," says Annie. "I liked seeing the bear," says Noah. "I just loved sharing this beautiful adventure with you guys," says Mom. Then Dad says, "I love this hot dog." Everyone busts out laughing while Dad takes a giant bite and closes his eyes.

The next morning, Annie and Mom put the tent down while Dad and Noah packed the gear up so they could hike down to the cabin.

Five miles later, with a few sunburns, and tired feet the family finally makes it back to the cabin. Everyone is so exhausted that they drop everything they carried on the floor and they all crawl in their beds. Dad says, "We better get some good rest because we have another adventure ahead of us tomorrow." And off they went to sleep.

Bright and early in the morning everyone is up ready to begin the day. Dad says, "Who is ready to see Old Faithful?" Noah asks, "What is that?" "Well, it is a geyser that sprays out of the earth every 1-2 hours and we are going to check it out, on that note let's all jump in the car."

As they enter the park, they check in at the Ranger station where the guide talks about the rules while in the park. The Ranger says, "Never ever touch the pools, they are too hot for our skin." Walking up the path to see Old Faithful the geyser begins to blow and it sprays at least 150 feet in the air. "Wow," the whole family said as they looked up.

Heading back to the cabin they stopped at the really old saloon called the Million Dollar Cowboy Bar in the small town of Jackson Hole. The whole family ordered the Cowboy favorite, the hamburger with fries. Once they finished their lunch, they made their way back to the cabin for one last campfire and a good night's sleep before making the journey home.

It was Dad and Annie's turn to build the fire tonight, so Dad taught Annie how to build a fire. As they sat around the fire telling stories of previous adventures, they knew that this would be one that they had fond memories of and would always be talked about. Dad says, "Off to bed, we have a long drive ahead of us tomorrow."

The following morning everyone looked as if they were busy bees packing all their gear into the car. "Before we leave, we must get a photo", says Dad. So, Dad asks the cabin neighbor to take a photo of the family. "Cheese, we love you Yellowstone."

Ten hours later they make it home safe and sound. As they pull into the driveway of their Home Sweet Home, Mom and Dad both say, "Until our next adventure."

THE END

www.ingramcontent.com/pod-product-compliance
Lightning Source LLC
Chambersburg PA
CBRC090825120626
46547CB00007B/605